second edition

Pupil Book

Blue Level

ROSE GRIFFITHS

Heinemann Educational Publishers
Halley Court, Jordan Hill, Oxford, OX2 8EJ
A part of Harcourt
www.myprimary.co.uk

Heinemann is a registered trademark of Harcourt Education Ltd

First edition first published 1996

Second edition first published 2005

10 09 08 07 06
10 9 8 7 6 5 4 3 2

ISBN 0 435 02142 7 / 978 0 43502 142 9

Designed and typeset by Susan Clarke
Illustrated by Tessa Richardson-Jones and Steve Smallman
Cover design by Susan Clarke
Printed and bound in China through Phoenix Offset

The author and publishers would like to thank teachers at the
following schools for their help in trialling these materials:
Murrayburn Primary School, Edinburgh
St Bernard's RC Primary School, Bristol
Plymouth Grove Primary School, Manchester
Lubenham Primary School, Leicester
St Peters CE Primary School, Leicester
St Peters CV Primary School, Gwent
Cawley Lane Junior School, West Yorkshire
Naphill and Walters Ash Combined School, High Wycombe
Emmer Green Primary School, Reading
St Anne's JMI School, Streetly

Contents

Using this book

Your teacher will talk to you about where you will start in *Number Connections*.

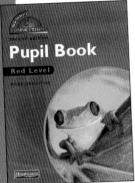    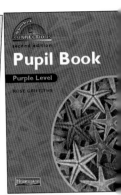

Getting started

Check that you <u>can</u> do the first two pages in each part of this book, before you do any more.

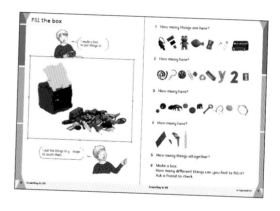

Reading

There are word lists in the *Teacher's Guide*.

These will help you learn any new words you need.

I've made cards from my list.

Extra activities

There are more activities and games in the *Copymasters* and the *Games Pack*.

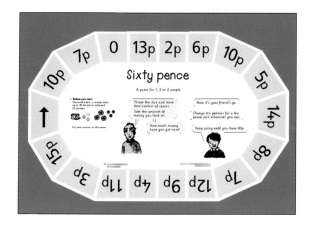

Take them home for extra practice!

We like doing the Speedy Sums.

Can we get more right, and get quicker?

Progress tests and Record sheets

These are in the *Teacher's Guide*.

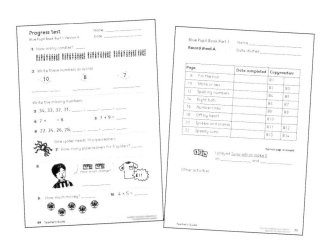

Check on your progress ...

and keep a record of what you've done!

Part 1
Contents

Counting and place value
Addition and subtraction
Multiplication and division

Fill the box

I made a box to put things in.

I put the things in groups to count them.

1 How many things are here?

2 How many here?

3 How many here?

4 How many here?

5 How many things altogether?

6 Make a box.
How many different things can you find to fill it?
Ask a friend to check.

More or less

I'm counting forwards.
1, 2, 3, 4, 5, …

I'm counting backwards.
12, 11, 10, 9, 8, …

Copy these. Write the next four numbers.

1 9, 10, 11, 12, …

2 10, 9, 8, 7, …

3 20, 21, 22, 23 …

4 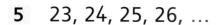 15, 14, 13, 12, …

5 23, 24, 25, 26, …

6 30, 29, 28, 27, …

7 23, 22, 21, 20 …

8 17, 16, 15, 14, …

9 35, 36, 37, 38, …

10 38, 39, 40, 41, …

11   What is one more than 13?

12   What is one more than 19?

13   What is one more than 37?

14   What is one more than 48?

15   What is one less than 16?

16   What is one less than 34?

Spelling numbers

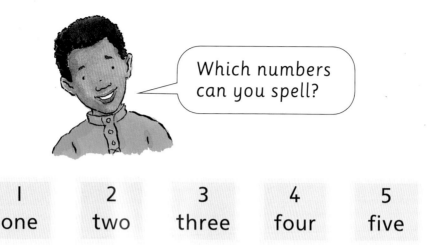

Which numbers can you spell?

1	2	3	4	5
one	two	three	four	five

Do these sums. Write the answers as words.

1 Four add one

2 Three add one

3 One add two

4 One add one

5 Two add two

6 Three add two

7 Two add one

8 Two add three

6	7	8	9	10
six	seven	eight	nine	ten

9 Four add four

10 Five add five

11 Three add four

12 Six add three

13 Three add three

14 Six add two

15 Seven add two

16 Six add one

Write the answers as words.

17 How many legs?

18 How many legs?

19 How many legs?

20 How many legs?

21 How many legs?

22 How many legs?

23 How many legs?

24 How many legs?

Eight bats

Count the bats.

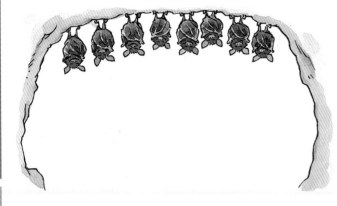

8 bats are sleeping.

No bats are flying.

8 + 0 = 8

1   How many are sleeping?

2   How many are flying?

3   7 + 1 =

4   How many are sleeping?

5   How many are flying?

6   6 + 2 =

7   How many are sleeping?

8   How many are flying?

9   5 + 3 =

10 How many are sleeping?

11 How many are flying?

12 $4 + 4 =$

13 How many are sleeping?

14 How many are flying?

15 $3 + 5 =$

16 How many are sleeping?

17 How many are flying?

18 $2 + 6 =$

19 How many are sleeping?

20 How many are flying?

21 $1 + 7 =$

22

No bats are sleeping.
How many are flying?

Number links

Here are 7 bricks.

4 red   3 yellow

What sums can you do with them?

1

4 + 3 =

2
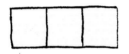

3 + 4 =

3
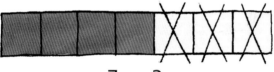

7 − 3 =

4
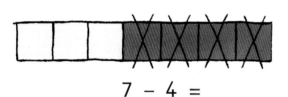

7 − 4 =

The numbers **3** **4** **7** are linked.

Use bricks.

1   **5**   **6**

 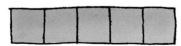

5   1 + 5   **7**   6 − 1

6   5 + 1   **8**   6 − 5

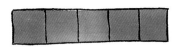   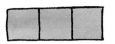

9 2 + 5   **13** 3 + 2

10 5 + 2   **14** 2 + 3

11 7 − 2   **15** 5 − 3

12 7 − 5   **16** 5 − 2

I can only make two sums because two numbers are the same.

17 3 + 3

18 6 − 3

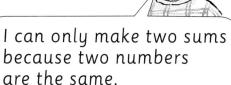

19 4 + 4

20 8 − 4

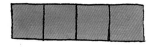 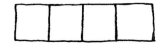

Off by heart

Which sums do you know off by heart?

2 add 2 makes 4

1 add 2 makes 3

If you do a sum lots of times,
you can learn the answer off by heart.

Copy and complete.

Ring any sums you know off by heart.

off by heart
$(2+1=3)$
2. $1+3=$

1 $2 + 1 =$

2 $1 + 3 =$

3 $0 + 5 =$

4 $3 + 0 =$

5 $1 + 2 =$

6 $4 + 0 =$

7 $2 + 2 =$

8 $3 + 1 =$

9 $2 + 3 =$

10 $4 + 1 =$

11 $1 + 4 =$

12 $3 + 2 =$

Now try with bigger numbers.

13 1 + 5 =   **17** 3 + 3 =   **21** 4 + 3 =

14 2 + 4 =   **18** 6 + 1 =   **22** 2 + 5 =

15 5 + 1 =   **19** 1 + 6 =   **23** 6 + 0 =

16 4 + 2 =   **20** 3 + 4 =   **24** 5 + 2 =

Do these sums make 7?
Write <u>Yes</u> or <u>No</u>.

25 5 + 2   **27** 2 + 6   **29** 4 + 1

26 4 + 3   **28** 3 + 4   **30** 6 + 1

Do these sums make 8?
Write <u>Yes</u> or <u>No</u>.

31 4 + 4   **33** 2 + 6

32 3 + 5   **34** 8 + 0

Ask your teacher if you can play
the 'Sums which make 8' game.

Spiders and snakes

You can make a spider with ten pipecleaners.

 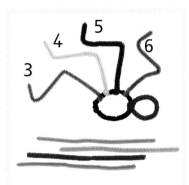 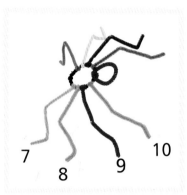

How many pipecleaners for:

1 2 spiders?

2 3 spiders?

3 4 spiders?

4 5 spiders?

How many spiders can you make with:

5 30 pipecleaners?

6 20 pipecleaners?

7 50 pipecleaners?

8 40 pipecleaners?

9 How many pipecleaners?

You can make a snake with two pipecleaners.

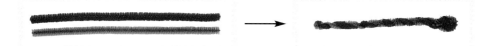

10 How many pipecleaners?

How many pipecleaners?

11

12

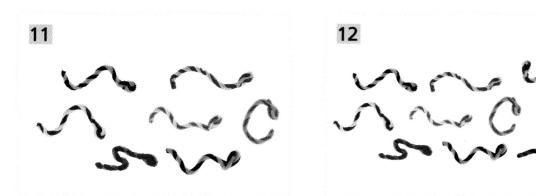

How many snakes can you make with:

13 20 pipecleaners? **14** 30 pipecleaners?

TEN

TEN

TEN

TEN

TEN

Speedy sums

 Use a stopwatch or a sand timer.

Can you get 10 sums right in 3 minutes?

1 2 + 4 =   **6** 1 + 4 =

2 1 + 7 =   **7** 3 + 3 =

3 5 + 3 =   **8** 6 + 2 =

4 4 + 0 =   **9** 4 + 3 =

5 2 + 2 =   **10** 0 + 3 =

 Check your answers. ✓ or ✗

 How many of these sums can you get right in 3 minutes?

1 7 − 2 =   **6** 3 − 1 =

2 4 − 1 =   **7** 4 − 3 =

3 8 − 4 =   **8** 2 − 2 =

4 5 − 3 =   **9** 7 − 4 =

5 6 − 5 =   **10** 6 − 2 =    ✓ or ✗

How many can you get right in 3 minutes?

1	4 + 2 =		**6**	5 − 1 =
2	6 − 4 =		**7**	3 + 5 =
3	7 + 0 =		**8**	7 − 3 =
4	4 − 2 =		**9**	6 + 1 =
5	1 + 5 =		**10**	3 − 3 =

Use Speedy Sums A made from Copymaster B13.

B13

Speedy sums Ⓐ
3 minute test

Name _____
Date _____

4 + 2 = ____   5 + 2 = ____   2 + 2 = ____
3 + 4 = ____   1 + 6 = ____   0 + 7 = ____
1 + 3 = ____   2 + 5 = ____   4 + 3 = ____
6 + 1 = ____   0 + 2 = ____   3 + 2 = ____
2 + 3 = ____   4 + 1 = ____   3 + 3 = ____
5 + 0 = ____   2 + 4 = ____   1 + 4 = ____
3 + 1 = ____   1 + 5 = ____   Score: ____

Mental recall of bonds within 8   ◄ Blue Pupil Book Part 1 pages 22 and 23   Number Connections © Rose Griffiths 2005 Harcourt Education Ltd

Can you get 20 sums right in 3 minutes?

Check your answers. ✓ or ✗
Count how many you got right.

Talk to your teacher about what to do next.

T-shirts

You can count up ...   or take away.

£6   +   £4 = £10

$$10 - 6 = 4$$

So there is £4 change.

1

£12

How much change?

2

£3

How much change?

3

£14

How much change?

 I bought 2 green t-shirts.

4 How much did I spend?

5  How much change?

 I bought a red t-shirt and 2 white ones.

6 How much did I spend?

7 How much change?

I bought a green t-shirt and a white one.

8 How much did I spend?

9 How much change?

10

What could I buy with £10?

Bowling

We made ten skittles. I put them like this.

From above they looked like this.

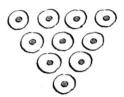

I knocked down 8 skittles. That's 2 still standing.

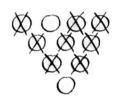

1  I knocked down 3 skittles.

How many still standing?

2 I knocked down 5 skittles.

How many still standing?

3  I knocked down 9 skittles.

How many still standing?

4  I knocked down 6 skittles. *4*

How many still standing?

5  I knocked down 1 skittle. *9*

How many still standing?

6  I knocked down 4 skittles. *6*

How many still standing?

7 I knocked down 2 skittles. *8*

How many still standing?

8 I knocked down 10 skittles!

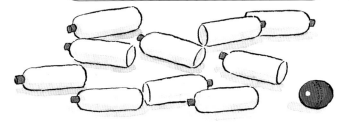  *0*

How many still standing?

9 I knocked down 7 skittles. *3*

How many still standing?

10 I didn't knock down any skittles. *Ø6*

How many still standing?

Fives and ones

This is 5p ...

and this is 5p.

How much money is in each box?

1

2

3

4

5

You need: 35p in 5p coins and 4p in 1p coins.

Make each amount with coins.
Draw it in your book.

Or print it, with coin stamps.

6 10p   **7** 7p   **8** 9p

9 16p   **10** 13p   **11** 18p

12 14p   **13** 20p   **14** 22p

15 27p   **16** 30p   **17** 29p

18 33p   **19** 35p   **20** 38p

Ask your teacher if you can play the 'Fifty pence' game.

Pick up bricks

Katrina picked up these bricks with one hand.

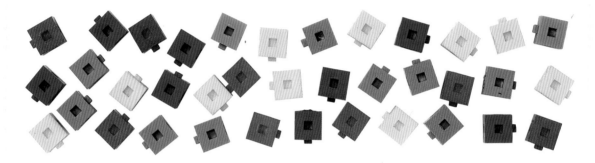

1   How many bricks?

I put the bricks in tens.
It's easier to count them.

2   How many bricks?

How many bricks?

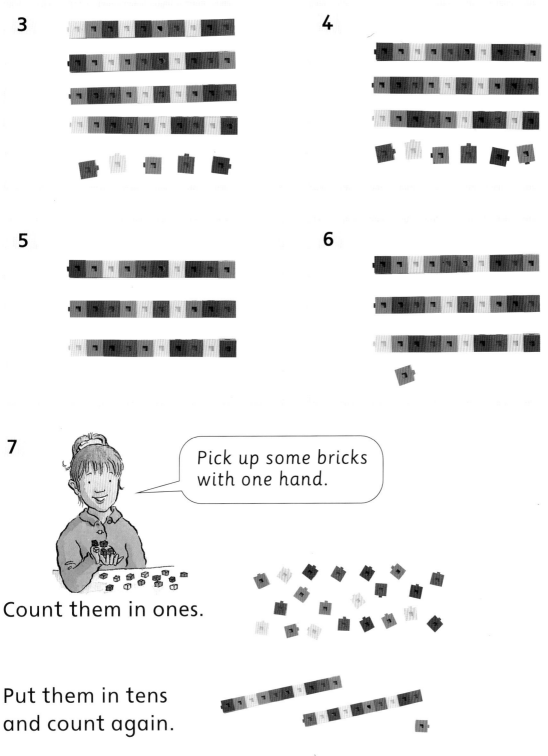

3

4

5

6

7

Pick up some bricks with one hand.

Count them in ones.

Put them in tens and count again.

Write how many you picked up.

Have three turns.

Bat and fives

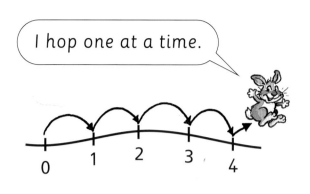

I hop one at a time.

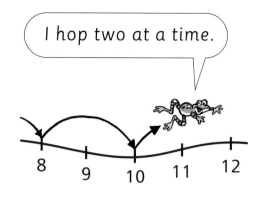

I hop two at a time.

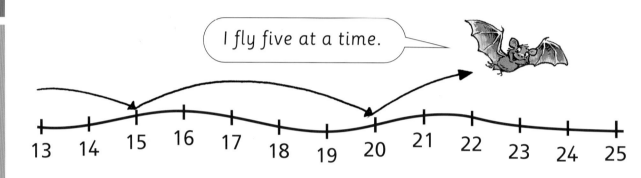

I fly five at a time.

Which number will I land on next?

1

2

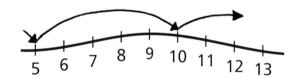

3

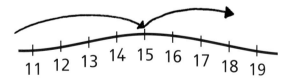

4

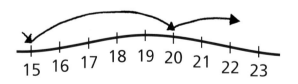

5

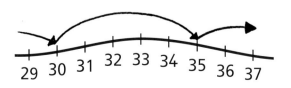

6

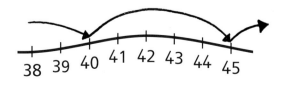

0, 5, 10, 15, 20, 25, 30, ...

... 35, 40, 45, 50, ...
These numbers are called <u>multiples of five</u>.

You can get <u>multiples of five</u> by adding fives, or by <u>multiplying</u> by five.

 Use a calculator.

Look for this button: ✕

7 5 + 5 + 5 =

8 3 × 5 =

That's 3 fives.

3 times 5

9 5 + 5 + 5 + 5 =

10 4 × 5 =

Multiples of 5 to 50 ▶ Copymasters B22 and B23 **33**

Card sums

I practise adding with playing cards.

I pick two cards and add them.

9 + 3 = 12

Check

Add these.

This counts as 1.

1

2

3

4

5

6

≈ Red and black ≈

A game for 2 people.

You need: a pack of playing cards, <u>without</u> the picture cards and a calculator.

Shuffle the red cards. Put them in a pile, face down.
Shuffle the black cards. Put them in a pile, face down.

Take a red card and a black card. Add them.

Your friend can check with a calculator.

If you are right, keep the cards. If not, put them back at the bottom of each pile.

Now it's your friend's go.

Keep going until all the cards have gone.

More card sums

Work with a friend if you want to.

You need
20 playing cards.

Find as many ways
as you can to make 12,
with a red card and
a black card.

Draw or write down each way.

Part 2
Contents

Counting and place value
Addition and subtraction
Multiplication and division

Coins in a jar

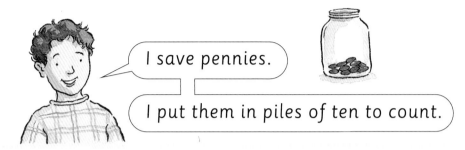

I save pennies.

I put them in piles of ten to count.

There is 34p here.

How much money?

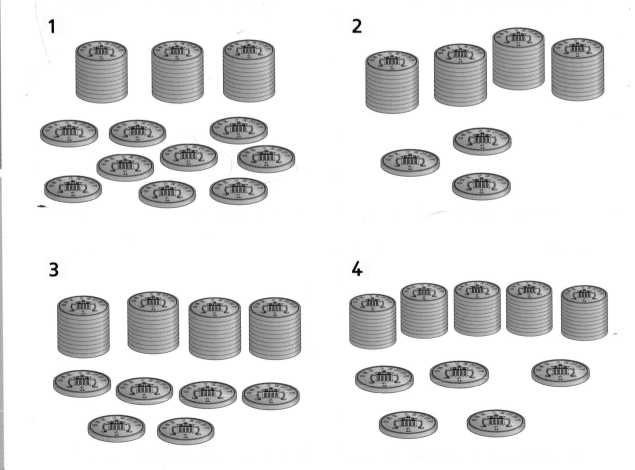

1

2

3

4

I save pennies _and_ ten pences.

As soon as I get 10 pennies,
I swap them for a ten pence coin.

How much money?

5

6

7

8

Ask your teacher if you can play
the 'Sixty pence' game.

Sums in words

Use sums to practise your spelling.

1   Copy these.

11 eleven	12 twelve	13 thirteen	14 fourteen	15 fifteen

Do these. Write the answers as words.

2   Ten add one   **3**   Ten add four

4   Ten add five   **5**   Six add six

6   Eight add five   **7**   Nine add two

8   Seven add seven   **9**   Ten add three

10      Eleven add one

11   Thirteen add two

12   Four add ten   **13**   Nine add three

Can you spell
<u>six</u>, <u>seven</u>, <u>eight</u> and <u>nine</u>?

Yes.

They help you spell <u>six</u>teen, <u>seven</u>teen, <u>eight</u>een
and <u>nine</u>teen.

14 Copy these.

16	17	18	19	20
sixteen	seventeen	eighteen	nineteen	twenty

Do these. Write the answers as words.

15 Eight add ten

16 Six add ten

17 Ten add ten

18 Eighteen add one

19 Seven add ten

20 Twelve add four

21 Nine add ten

22 Sixteen add one

23

Seventeen add one

24 Fifteen add five

Tens and ones

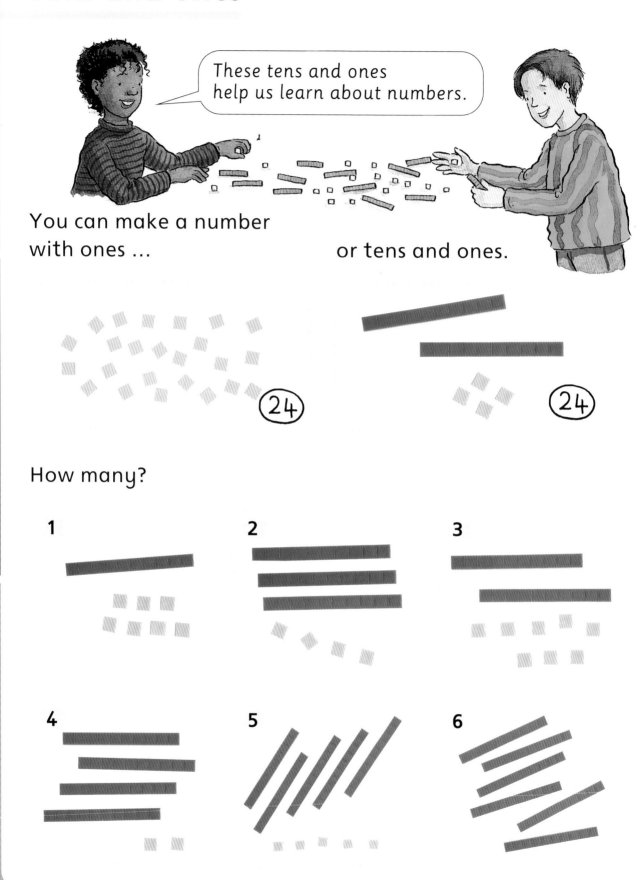

These tens and ones help us learn about numbers.

You can make a number with ones ...

or tens and ones.

24

24

How many?

1

2

3

4

5

6

Work with a friend.

Make each number
with tens and ones.

I'll check
your number.

Yes, that's 23.

Then draw it.

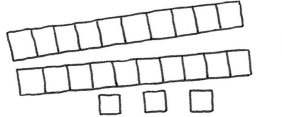

| 23 |

7 | 12 | 8 | 43 | 9 | 26 | 10 | 37 |

11 | 50 | 12 | 59 | 13 | 41 | 14 | 35 |

15 | 28 | 16 | 17 | 17 | 36 | 18 | 54 |

Ask your teacher if you can play
the 'Tens and ones' game.

Two times table

0, 2, 4, 6, 8, 10, 12, ...

These numbers are called <u>multiples of two</u>.

You can get <u>multiples of two</u> by adding twos, or by <u>multiplying</u> by two.

One bird

1 How many legs?

2 $1 \times 2 =$

Two birds

3 How many legs?

4 2 + 2

5 $2 \times 2 =$

Three birds

6 How many legs?

7 2 + 2 + 2

8 $3 \times 2 =$

Four birds

9 How many legs?

10 2 + 2 + 2 + 2

11 $4 \times 2 =$

Five birds

Six birds

12 How many legs?

13 2 + 2 + 2 + 2 + 2

14 5 × 2 =

15 How many legs?

16 2 + 2 + 2 + 2 + 2 + 2

17 6 × 2 =

Seven birds

Sixteen legs!

18 How many legs?

19 2 + 2 + 2 + 2 + 2 + 2 + 2

20 7 × 2 =

21 How many birds?

22 2 + 2 + 2 + 2 + 2 + 2 + 2 + 2

23 8 × 2 =

24 Copy and complete.

Two times table

0 × 2 =	4 × 2 =	8 × 2 =
1 × 2 =	5 × 2 =	9 × 2 =
2 × 2 =	6 × 2 =	10 × 2 =
3 × 2 =	7 × 2 =	

Hours and half hours

I dropped my clock! The big hand fell off.

You can still use it to tell the time for hours and half hours.

Does the clock say 2 o'clock? Write <u>Yes</u> or <u>No</u>.

1

2

3

What's the time?

4 o'clock

What is the time?

4

5

6

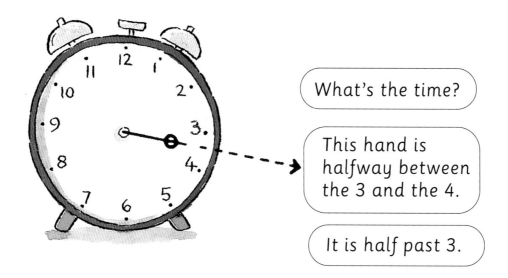

What's the time?

This hand is halfway between the 3 and the 4.

It is half past 3.

What is the time?

7

8

9

10

11

12

Use a real clock (with 2 hands!).

13 Make the clock say 3 o'clock. Draw it.

14 Make the clock say half past 3. Draw it.

Nine counters

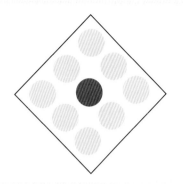

No red counters. 9 yellow counters. $0 + 9 = 9$

1 How many red counters?

2 How many yellow counters?

3 $1 + 8 =$

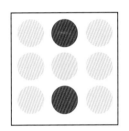

4 How many red?

5 How many yellow?

6 $2 + 7 =$

7 How many red?

8 How many yellow?

9 $3 + 6 =$

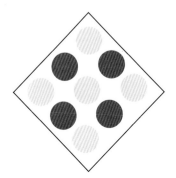

10 How many red?

11 How many yellow?

12 $4 + 5 =$

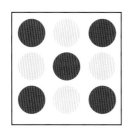

13 How many red counters?

14 How many yellow counters?

15 $\boxed{5} \; \boxed{+} \; \boxed{4} \; \boxed{=}$

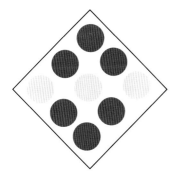

16 How many red?

17 How many yellow?

18 $\boxed{6} \; \boxed{+} \; \boxed{3} \; \boxed{=}$

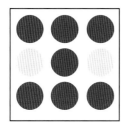

19 How many red?

20 How many yellow?

21 $\boxed{7} \; \boxed{+} \; \boxed{2} \; \boxed{=}$

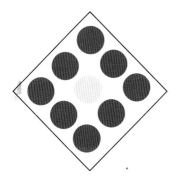

22 How many red?

23 How many yellow?

24 $\boxed{8} \; \boxed{+} \; \boxed{1} \; \boxed{=}$

Ask your teacher
if you can play the 'Make 9' game.

Fives and tens

This is 10p ...   and this is 10p.

How much money is in each box?

1

2

3

4

You can swap 4 fives …   for 2 tens.

5 6 fives … How many tens?

6 8 fives … How many tens?

7 10 fives … How many tens?

          8 One ten … How many fives?

9 5 tens … How many fives?

10 How can you make 50p
with fives and tens?

Draw all the ways.

Here's one way.

Speedy sums

You can do sums quickly
if you learn them off by heart.

Copy and
complete.

Ring any sums
you know off by heart.

1	2 + 2 =	**5**	6 + 1 =	**9** 3 + 2 =
2	4 + 1 =	**6**	4 + 4 =	**10** 0 + 1 =
3	5 + 2 =	**7**	1 + 3 =	**11** 1 + 1 =
4	3 + 3 =	**8**	1 + 6 =	**12** 0 + 2 =

13 2 + 4 =   **17** 1 + 2 =

14 2 + 1 =   **18** 5 + 1 =

15 4 + 0 =   **19** 3 + 0 =

16 2 + 3 =   **20** 3 + 4 =

✓ or ✗

Do these make 8?
Write <u>Yes</u> or <u>No</u>.

21 $4 + 4$ **23** $0 + 8$ **25** $1 + 6$

22 $5 + 2$ **24** $3 + 6$ **26** $2 + 6$

Do these make 5?
Write <u>Yes</u> or <u>No</u>.

27 $6 - 1$ **30** $8 - 3$ **33** $5 - 0$

28 $9 - 4$ **31** $7 - 3$ **34** $5 - 5$

29 $8 - 0$ **32** $6 - 2$ **35** $9 - 2$

Use a stopwatch
or a sand timer.

Use Speedy sums E
made from Copymaster B44.

Speedy sums E
1 2 3 minute test
Name _____
Date _____
B44

$5 + 2 =$ ___	$8 - 3 =$ ___	$3 + 3 =$ ___
$2 + 3 =$ ___	$7 - 6 =$ ___	$5 - 3 =$ ___
$4 + 4 =$ ___	$3 - 3 =$ ___	$4 + 5 =$ ___
$5 + 0 =$ ___	$9 - 5 =$ ___	$8 - 2 =$ ___
$1 + 8 =$ ___	$7 - 2 =$ ___	$3 + 4 =$ ___
$6 + 3 =$ ___	$2 - 1 =$ ___	$6 - 4 =$ ___
$2 + 4 =$ ___	$9 - 2 =$ ___	Score: ___

Mental recall of bonds within 9

Can you get
20 sums right
in 3 minutes?

Check your answers. ✓ or ✗
Count how many you got right.

Talk to your teacher
about what to do next.

Boxes

Shaun and Emma are playing 'Boxes'.

We take turns to draw a line.

If my line makes a box, I put my letter in it ...

and draw another line.

1st game

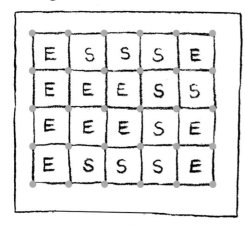

Emma got 11 boxes.
Shaun got 9.

1 Who won, Emma or Shaun?

2 How many boxes altogether?

1 1 + 9 =

2nd game

S	S	S	S	S
S	E	S	S	S
E	E	S	S	S
E	E	S	S	S

3 How many boxes for Emma?

4 How many for Shaun?

5 How many boxes altogether?

6 Who won?

3rd game

I got
10 boxes.

E	E	S	E	E
S	S	E	E	E
S	S	S	S	E
S	S	E	S	E

No, that's not right.
I got 11 boxes.
11 + 10 does <u>not</u>
make 20.

7 How many boxes for Emma?

8 How many for Shaun?

9 How many boxes altogether?

10 Who won?

4th game

I got 12 boxes.

11 How many boxes for Shaun?

12 Who won?

Teen numbers

Thirteen

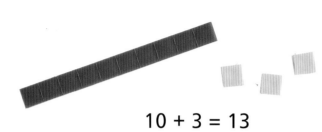

10 + 3 = 13

Make each number
with a ten and ones.

Fourteen

Nineteen

Sixteen

Fifteen

Eighteen

Copy and complete.

1   10 + 4 =

2   4 + 10 =

3   10 + 9 =

4   9 + 10 =

5   10 + 6 =

6   6 + 10 =

7   10 + 5 =

8   5 + 10 =

9   10 + 8 =

10 8 + 10 =

 ✓ or ✗

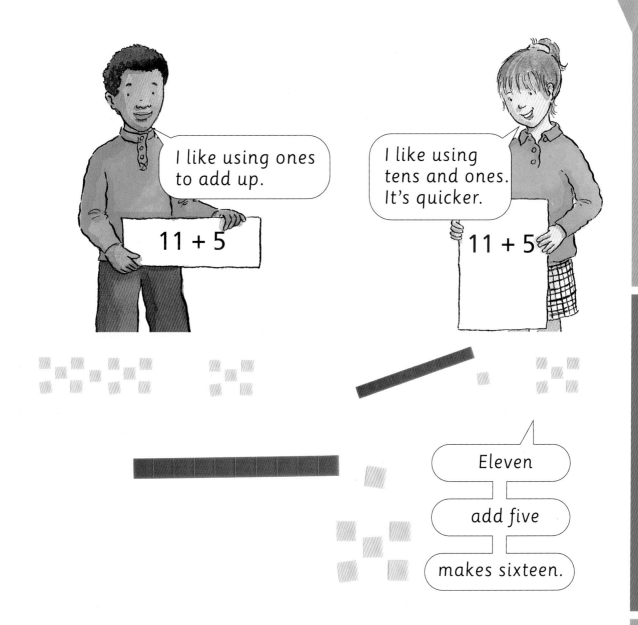

Use tens and ones. Copy and complete.

11 $15 + 2 =$ **15** $14 + 3 =$

12 $10 + 4 =$ **16** $11 + 6 =$

13 $12 + 6 =$ **17** $13 + 2 =$

14 $11 + 4 =$ **18** $12 + 4 =$

Five times table

0, 5, 10, 15, 20, 25, ...

These numbers are called <u>multiples of five</u>.

You can get <u>multiples of five</u> by adding fives,
or by <u>multiplying</u> by five.

One starfish

1 How many legs?

2  = 5

Two starfish

3 How many legs?

4 5 + 5 = 10

5  = 10

Three starfish

6 How many legs?

7 5 + 5 + 5 = 15

8  = 15

Four starfish

9 How many legs?

10 5 + 5 + 5 + 5 = 20

11  = 20

Five starfish

12 How many legs?

13 5 + 5 + 5 + 5 + 5 = 25

14 $\boxed{5} \times \boxed{5} =$ 25

Six starfish

15 How many legs?

16 5 + 5 + 5 + 5 + 5 + 5 = 30

17 $\boxed{6} \times \boxed{5} =$ 30

Eight starfish behind a rock.

Seven starfish

18 How many legs?

19 5 + 5 + 5 + 5 + 5 + 5 + 5 = 35

20 $\boxed{7} \times \boxed{5} =$ 35

21 How many legs?

22 5 + 5 + 5 + 5 + 5 + 5 + 5 + 5

23 $\boxed{8} \times \boxed{5} =$

24 Copy and complete.

Five times table

0 × 5 = 5	4 × 5 = 20	8 × 5 = 40
1 × 5 = 5	5 × 5 = 25	9 × 5 = 45
2 × 5 = 10	6 × 5 = 30	10 × 5 = 50
3 × 5 = 15	7 × 5 = 35	

More teen numbers

What's sixteen take away ten?

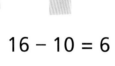

Six

$16 - 10 = 6$

Make each number with a ten and ones.

Fifteen

Thirteen

Seventeen

Nineteen

Copy and complete.

1 $15 - 10 =$

2 $15 - 5 =$

3 $13 - 10 =$

4 $13 - 3 =$

5 $17 - 10 =$

6 $17 - 7 =$

7 $19 - 10 =$

8 $19 - 9 =$

 ✓ or ✗

Eighteen

take away four

is fourteen.

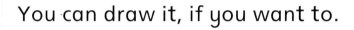

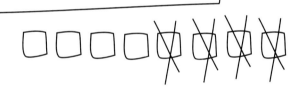

You can draw it, if you want to.

18 – 4 = 14

Use tens and ones. Copy and complete.

9 18 – 3 =   13 19 – 7 =

10 14 – 10 =   14 13 – 2 =

11 17 – 6 =   15 16 – 1 =

12 15 – 5 =   16 18 – 11 =

 ✓ or ✗

Photos

I can take 24 photos with this film.

1

I've taken 2 photos.

How many more can I take?

2

Now I've taken 4 photos.

How many more can I take?

3

Now I've taken 12 photos.

How many more can I take?

4

Now I've taken 17 photos.

How many more can I take?

5

Now I've taken 20 photos.

How many more can I take?

6

Now I've taken 24 photos.

How many more can I take?

You took 14 photos of your cat,
2 photos of your finger,
and 8 photos of me!

7 Check the total. 14 + 2 + 8

8

These all make 24.

14 + 2 + 8 = 24
12 + 12 = 24
20 + 4 = 24
10 + 10 + 4 = 24

Write ten more sums which make 24.

Ask a friend to check. ✓ or ✗

Hopping frogs

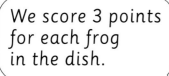

We score 3 points for each frog in the dish.

3 + 3 + 3 = 9

9 points

What did we score?

1

2 frogs in the dish.

3 + 3 = ____

2

4 frogs in the dish.

3

5 frogs in the dish.

What did we score?

4

None in.

5

6 frogs in the dish.

6

I scored 12 points.

How many frogs in the dish?

7 I scored 3. How many frogs in the dish?

8 I scored 9. How many frogs in the dish?

9 I scored 15. How many frogs in the dish?

10 I scored 6. How many frogs in the dish?

Make £15

Work with a friend if you want to.
Make a £10 note and three £5 notes.
Collect fifteen '£1 coins'.  or

Find as many ways as you can to make £15.

Draw each way.

This is one way.

Part 3
Contents

Counting and place value
Addition and subtraction
Multiplication and division
Mixed problems

Joke shop

Can you find the joke biscuit?

1   How many biscuits altogether?

I bought
a packet of joke ants!

2 How many ants altogether?

Tens and teens

Use sums to practise your spelling.

1   Copy these.

30	40	50	60	70
thirty	forty	fifty	sixty	seventy

Do these. Write the answers as words.

2   Twenty add ten

3   Forty add ten

4   Thirty add ten

5   Forty add twenty

6   Ten add twenty

7   Ten add sixty

8

Thirty add twenty

9   Fifty add twenty

10   Thirty add thirty

11   Twenty add twenty

12   Ten add ten add ten

13   Fifty add ten

4	4th	14	40
four	fourth	fourteen	forty

Forty does not have a <u>u</u>.

Write these numbers as words.

14 **4**   15 **14**   16 **40**   17 **4th**

When you say **13** and **30** , the first part sounds the same.

Work with a friend.
Say these out loud, then write the numbers as words.

18 **17** and **70**   19 **15** and **50**

20 **14** and **40**   21 **16** and **60**

22 **13** and **30**

Ask your teacher if you can play 'Tens and teens bingo'.

What comes next?

2, 4, 6, 8, 10, 12, ...

You're counting in twos.

Copy these. Write the next three numbers.

1 10, 12, 14, 16, ...

2 16, 14, 12, 10, ...

3 22, 24, 26, 28, ...

4 26, 28, 30, 32, ...

5

30, 28, 26, 24, ...

6 38, 40, 42, 44, ...

7 40, 38, 36, 34, ...

8 16, 18, 20, 22, ...

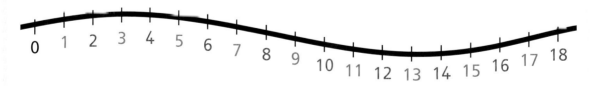

0 1 2 3 4 5 6 7 8 9 10 11 12 13 14 15 16 17 18

The red numbers are called <u>even</u> numbers.

9 What are the blue numbers called?

I'm counting in fives.
5, 10, 15, 20, 25, ...

Copy these. Write the next six numbers.

10 5, 10, 15, 20, ...

11 50, 45, 40, 35, ...

12

What am I counting in?
10, 20, 30, 40, 50, 60, ...

Counting backwards is harder than counting forwards.

Practise with a friend.

<u>Count out loud</u> from 20 down to 0 in twos.
Your friend can check.

20 18 16 14 12 10 8 6 4 2 0

<u>Count out loud</u> from 50 down to 0 in fives.
Your friend can check.

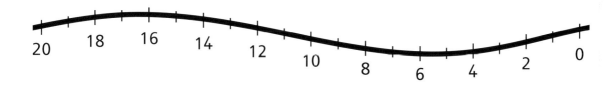

50 45 40 35 30 25 20 15 10 5 0

Footballs

£9, please.

Copy and complete.

1 How much change?

2 $10 - 9 =$

3 $9 + \boxed{} = 10$

£8, please.

4 How much change?

5 $10 - 8 =$

6 $8 + \boxed{} = 10$

£7, please.

7 How much change?

8 $10 - 7 =$

9 $7 + \boxed{} = 10$

£6, please.

10 How much change?

Copy and complete.

11 $10 - 6 =$

12 $6 + \boxed{} = 10$

£5, please.

13 How much change?

14 $10 - 5 =$

15 $5 + \boxed{} = 10$

Copy and complete.

16 $10 - 4 =$

17 $4 + \boxed{} = 10$

18 $10 - 3 =$

19 $3 + \boxed{} = 10$

20 $10 - 2 =$

21 $2 + \boxed{} = 10$

22 $10 - 1 =$

23 $1 + \boxed{} = 10$

Ask your teacher if you can play
the 'Sums which make 10' game.

Easier adding

You can add up in any order.

Copy and complete.

1 8 + 2   **3** 2 + 13   **5** 15 + 4

2 2 + 8   **4** 13 + 2   **6** 4 + 15

I put the bigger number first ...

because I think it's easier.

I do this ...

11 + 3

11.....................add 3... makes 14

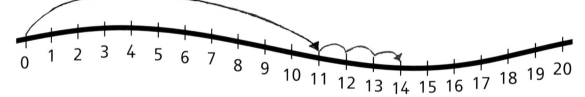

not this.

3 + 11

3......................add 11.............. makes 14

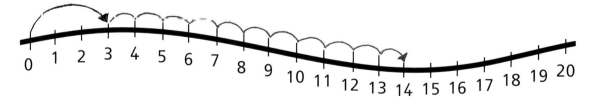

Which way do <u>you</u> think is easier?
Talk to your teacher about it.

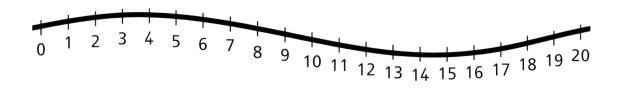

0 1 2 3 4 5 6 7 8 9 10 11 12 13 14 15 16 17 18 19 20

Put the biggest number first.
Use the number line if you want to.

7 4 + 12

8 3 + 16

9 12 + 7

10 8 + 9

11 1 + 16

12 9 + 4

13 2 + 4 + 13

14 7 + 9 + 2

15 1 + 12 + 1

16 5 + 2 + 9

17 4 + 1 + 8

18 1 + 14 + 5

Sometimes you can find <u>tens</u>
when you add up 3 numbers.

8 + 7 + 2

8 add 2 makes 10.
10 add 7 makes 17.

Look for tens. Copy and complete.

19 5 + 4 + 5

20 6 + 1 + 9

21 3 + 13 + 6

22 4 + 9 + 6

23 2 + 9 + 8

24 7 + 4 + 6

Speedy sums

Work with a friend.

Write question numbers 1 to 20.
Ask your friend to read the questions to you.

Write your answers
as quickly as you can.

1	2 + 8	**8**	7 − 1	**15**	1 + 5
2	0 + 4	**9**	10 − 4	**16**	8 − 6
3	6 + 3	**10**	3 − 0	**17**	4 + 4
4	5 + 5	**11**	6 − 3	**18**	10 − 3
5	2 + 5	**12**	7 − 4	**19**	7 + 2
6	1 + 9	**13**	4 − 2	**20**	9 − 8
7	3 + 5	**14**	9 − 4		

 ✓ or ✗

Now <u>you</u> read the questions
to your friend.

Do these make 10?
Write <u>Yes</u> or <u>No</u>.

21 $0 + 10$ **23** $3 + 7$ **25** $8 + 1$

22 $2 + 7$ **24** $5 + 5$ **26** $6 + 4$

Do these make 7?
Write <u>Yes</u> or <u>No</u>.

27 $3 + 4$ **30** $9 - 2$ **33** $8 - 2$

28 $6 + 2$ **31** $1 + 6$ **34** $7 - 0$

29 $10 - 3$ **32** $5 + 2$ **35** $4 + 3$

Use a stopwatch
or a sand timer.

Use Speedy sums G
made from Copymaster B71.

Can you get
20 sums right
in 3 minutes?

Check your answers. ✓ or ✗
Count how many you got right.

Talk to your teacher
about what to do next.

Adding up

Use tens and ones.

Fourteen add twelve is ten add ten and four add two.

$$14 + 12 = 26$$

Add up the tens ... and add up the ones.

Use tens and ones. Copy and complete.

1 12 + 17

2 20 + 6

3 13 + 13

4 15 + 14

5 11 + 15

6 23 + 6

7 16 + 10

8 18 + 11

9 10 + 15

10 15 + 12

Sometimes when you add up, you will have ten ones, or more!

You can swap ten ones for a ten, if you want to.

Do this with tens and ones.

15 + 17

Swap!

5 add 5 makes another ten

15 + 17 = 32

Use tens and ones. Copy and complete.

11 17 + 11   **12** 20 + 8   **13** 16 + 18

14 21 + 15   **15** 17 + 16   **16** 20 + 19

Three times table

0, 3, 6, 9, 12, 15, 18, ...

These numbers are called <u>multiples of three</u>.

You can get <u>multiples of three</u> by adding threes, or by <u>multiplying</u> by three.

One layer of bricks

1 How many bricks?

2 $\boxed{1} \times \boxed{3} =$

Three layers of bricks

3 How many bricks?

4 3 + 3 + 3

5 $\boxed{3} \times \boxed{3} =$

Five layers of bricks

6 How many bricks?

7 3 + 3 + 3 + 3 + 3

8 $\boxed{5} \times \boxed{3} =$

Seven layers of bricks

9 How many bricks?

10 3 + 3 + 3 + 3 + 3 + 3 + 3

11 $\boxed{7} \times \boxed{3} =$

Eight layers of bricks

12 How many bricks?

13 3 + 3 + 3 + 3 + 3 + 3 + 3 + 3

14 8 × 3 =

Nine layers of bricks ⟶

15 How many bricks?

16 3 + 3 + 3 + 3 + 3 + 3 + 3 + 3 + 3

17 9 × 3 =

Thirty bricks!

18 How many layers?

19 3 + 3 + 3 + 3 + 3 + 3 + 3 + 3 + 3 + 3

20 ☐ × 3 = 30

21 Copy and complete.

Three times table

0 × 3 =	4 × 3 =	8 × 3 =
1 × 3 =	5 × 3 =	9 × 3 =
2 × 3 =	6 × 3 =	10 × 3 =
3 × 3 =	7 × 3 =	

Fifty pences

This is 50p ...   and this is 50p.

1 How many 10p coins make 50p?
Draw them or print them.

2 How many 5p coins make 50p?
Draw them or print them.

3
> How many 2p coins make 50p?

Use coins.

How much money is in each box?

4

5

6

This is £1 ...

and this is £1.

How much money is in each box?

7

8

9

This is
one pound fifty ...

and so is this.

£1·50

How much money is in each box?

10

11

12

Dog's toys

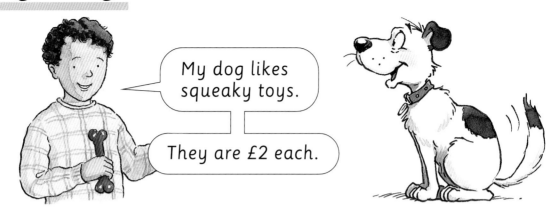

1 How much for 3 toys?

2 $3 \times 2 =$

3 How much for 5 toys?

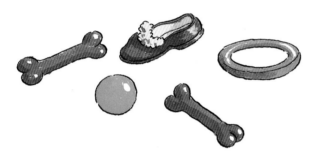

4 $5 \times 2 =$

5 How much for 8 toys?

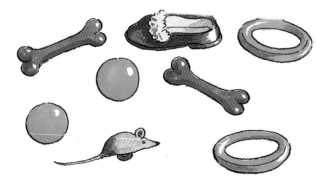

6 $8 \times 2 =$

I spent £6.

How many toys did she buy?

How many 2s make 6?

6 ÷ 2 = 3

↑
divided by

3 toys!

I spent £8.

7 How many toys?

8 8 ÷ 2 =

I spent £12.

9 How many toys?

10 1 2 ÷ 2 =

Swimming

Holiday Special

Junior swim   50p
Adult swim   £1·00

3 juniors please.

That's £1·50 altogether.

How much will it cost?

1 2 juniors, please.

2 2 adults and 2 juniors, please.

3 1 adult and 3 juniors, please.

4 4 juniors and 2 adults, please.

5 1 adult and 1 junior, please.

6 5 juniors, please.

7 2 adults and 3 juniors, please.

8 1 adult and 2 juniors, please.

We put our clothes in lockers.

Do Copymaster B80.
Then answer these questions.

9

My locker is number 28.

My locker is under yours.
Which locker is mine?

10

I want a locker on the top row.

Which lockers can I use?

11

I want a locker with a 6 on it.

Which lockers can I use?

12

Our lockers are next to each other.

They add up to 9.

Which lockers are they?

Dog food

My dog eats 2 tins of food a day.

In 3 days, she eats <u>3 lots</u> of 2 tins.

$3 \times 2 = 6$ 6 tins

1 How many tins in 4 days?

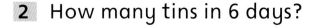

4 lots of 2 — 4 times 2 — 4×2

2 How many tins in 6 days?

3 How many tins in 2 days?

4 How many tins in 7 days?

5 How many tins in 5 days?

6 How many tins in 8 days?

7 How many tins in 9 days?

8 How many tins in 10 days?

 ✓ or ✗

9 How many days will 10 tins last?

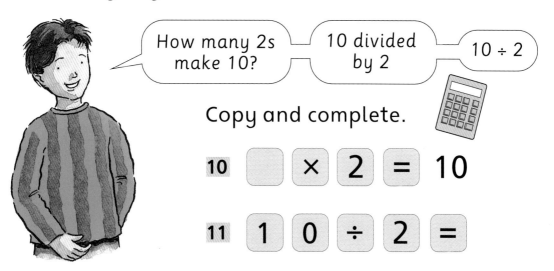

How many 2s make 10? — 10 divided by 2 — $10 \div 2$

Copy and complete.

10 ☐ × 2 = 10

11 1 0 ÷ 2 =

12 How many days will 14 tins last?

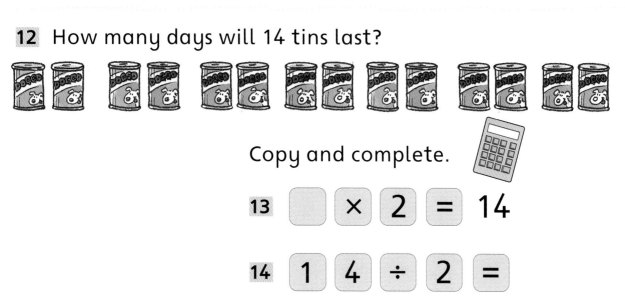

Copy and complete.

13 ☐ × 2 = 14

14 1 4 ÷ 2 =

Taking away

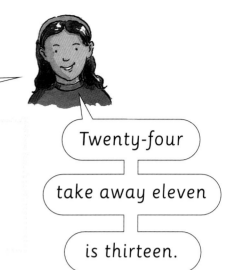

Use tens and ones.

Twenty-four take away eleven is thirteen.

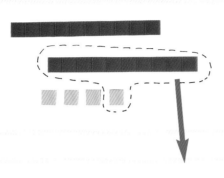

$$24 + 11 = 13$$

Make each number with tens and ones.

Thirty-six

Twenty-nine

Nineteen

Twenty-six

Thirty-three

Copy and complete.

1 36 – 14

2 29 – 17

3 19 – 18

4 26 – 13

5 33 – 13

I had 34p.
I spent 12p on an ice pop.

So you had 22p left!

$$34p - 12p = 22p$$

Use tens and ones.

How much did each person have left?

6

I had 28p.
I spent 15p.

7

I had 25p.
I spent 15p.

8

I had 32p.
I spent 15p.

9

I had 40p.
I spent 13p.

Talk to your teacher about how you did questions **8** and **9**.

Secret numbers

You need cards numbered 1 to 20.

I'm thinking of a number. It is smaller than 11.

1 2 3 4 5 6 7 8 9 10

It is bigger than 7.

8 9 10

It is an odd number.

It's 9

Find the secret numbers. Use cards.

1

I'm thinking of a number.
It is smaller than 9.
It is bigger than 5.

It is a multiple of 3.

2

I'm thinking of a number.
It is smaller than 15.
It is bigger than 12.

It is an even number.

3

I'm thinking of a number.
It is bigger than 10.
It is smaller than 18.

It is a multiple of 5.

4

I'm thinking of a number.
It is bigger than 6.
It is smaller than 11.

It is a multiple of 5.

5

I'm thinking of a number.
It is smaller than 17.
It is bigger than 7.

It is a multiple of 10.

6

I'm thinking of a number.
It is smaller than 19.
It is bigger than 15.

It is a multiple of 3.

Make a dozen

A <u>dozen</u> is twelve.

Find as many ways as you can to make 12.

You can add, take away, or multiply.

Write each way.

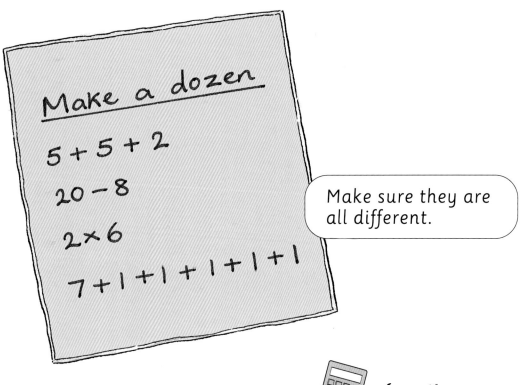

Make a dozen

5 + 5 + 2

20 − 8

2 × 6

7 + 1 + 1 + 1 + 1 + 1

Make sure they are all different.

Ask a friend to check.   ✓ or ✗